BEULAHLAND

VISIONARY PROSE AND POETRY

BY

D. F. HOWARD

ISBN: 0-7596-9130-4 (e-book)
ISBN: 0-7596-9131-2 (Paperback)
ISBN: 1-4107-4468-X (Dust Jacket)

This book is printed on acid-free paper.

1stBooks – rev. 02/11/04

Acknowledgments

I would like to thank everyone in support of my first literary offering. Also, I would like to add appreciation for my mother. Her love and rapport have prompted the person that I am today. Her investment in my life continues to endow my character and encourage my sense of being. Equally, I am grateful for the blessing of my father. His commitment and intuitiveness have inspired my convictions to serve while abiding God's ordinance and grace. Complementing his decency is his endless capacity of love conveyed to his family. I am honored to have inherited this quality. It is the energy that I preserve for anyone who strives to keep poised the intentions for integrity and respect in society. Lastly, I would like to thank Sula Janet Evans of Rutgers University for her editing advisements during the initial stages of this book.

CONTENTS

Foreword

This book is attributed towards the healing of generational curses.

_In most respects, this book is a portrayal
of humanity's submission to God._

_This coupling has revealed the fulfillment of my individual
purpose with the "promise" latent in everyman._

_What is more, the procession of these writings suggests
the beauty of conversation between creature and Creator._

Author's Note

The vocation to write this book has been a resolution for the disinclined part of me. In some cases, this is my testimony. Likewise, it is my divinely-coupled insight into many happenings under the sun. The pursuit of this expression is primarily credited to my obedience in God. It has ameliorated me from the reprobate interpretations of life into that of an understanding (pregnant with responsibility) portioned throughout my being. It is a testament of faith in all that is Holy. Beulahland is my "peace." A literary platform exhibiting the pain, joy and hidden blessings related to living. Inasmuch, it is my personal admittance of compassion for all people. The composition is intended as a therapeutic libation guided by the Holy Spirit; as suggested in the prose poem Mothering: Seeds of Three Through Ether. In the same way, it is an affirmation of my mother's mother. It was conceived in the admonition of our forefathers. More than that, the intent is to celebrate our ancestors who followed in the image of Christ; thereby, nourishing our totality and enabling each of us to find the way with an unfiltered birthright of love.

This book is dedicated in loving memory of

Barrett Boyd Howard

To Tirzah

You, Judah, shall no more be termed forsaken; nor shall your land be called desolate anymore. But you shall be called Hephzibah (my delight is in her) and you shall be called Beulah (married); for the Lord delights in you, and your land shall be married (owned and protected by the Lord).

-Isaiah 62:4

PART ONE

SUMMER BENDS TO FALL

~

CROSSROADS

THE REFORMER

Until the last second he was scorned

The fiend who worships himself untapped

The fiend who once sang the song of the living

Now buried alive

He reaps of his ring broken

Engagement broken

Marriage broken

Humanity broken

Image broken

Now Left

He is the token that once was the Living Word

Promised to be spoken

The fiend now sneers at his stagnant bravery

The fiend knows to make firm his grip

That once upheld the inherited torch well-lit

After much longing

The fiend entreats his loom to weave

Again

Potted-by-the-potter

Newly adorned

The fiend reforms

. . .

Vaguely remembering

He looks on

Upon his scorn

Finally bored with being born

D. F. Howard

ILLUSIONS
(overcoming through submission)

Once in a blue moon

I'd do it

Quite deliberately

I would approach it

I would cast my shadow over the insurmountable

The one thing that would never leave

That would always give me what I'd need

I'd allow it

It never having abused me

I'd see myself headed down that path

I would look at it dead on

I'd glorify it

Hesitate but I'd investigate it

I can recall how I tried to forget it

Two blue moons ago I even made a wager

(With myself of course just in case I couldn't do it)

To somehow shake it

But when I did bet against it

It took a part of me

The sacred vow I needed

It seduced my fidelity

Defeated

There I stood

The angry victim

Typical

So I chose not to become a philosopher

Lending theories as to why I'd done it

I only meant to go under long enough

To live through my listlessness

Again and again

Until I was there

Centered in the sublime

Livin' the so-called life

And so I began to harmonize like 14 Doo Wop guys

...

The following morning enveloped my bed

Flooded it red

The brightest daylight infiltrating my head

Like the reddest sun on it's wedding night

Having consummated their perfectness quite right

There lay the sun and his bride

Newly-torn

There they lay

Abed

Complacent

Flushed with crimson

The bed and their faces

No evidence of displacement in their relations

D. F. Howard

My situation was quite plain

I was no longer alone

I lay stock-still

Captured by the nourishment that the sun-light instilled

I was Home

No longer would I be disowned

All that while

I fought to strip away the rose-colored charisma housing my rage

My infatuation entertained that part of me

Determined to defy me

It wanted me senseless and given to a quiet death

That would excuse all my inadequacies

And any meandering glimpses of triumph

It had one place for me

That old indemnity I had presumed insurmountable

Can no longer deceive me with ill- tended maladies

I am beginning to understand solemnity

much more than that occasional moon

Much sooner than soon

BEARER OF THE BONE

(the power of forgiveness)

Dumpsite for your incredible feast

2 Gazelles

Wildebeests

Sandpipers

Tigers

5 willing beasts

Their brittle bone

Covering the land

Handsome molars

Big ones

Little ones

The newest ones

These two-legged ones

Chosen with certain ease

They are centuries old

Though you told

No guilt of yours was felt

Alas

It comes to pass

Though you told

(words to bold)

That killing was not the appropriate name

Several relaxed words distilling your eventual shame

Today that disclaimed truth

100 proof

Now sickens you

As you lick your wounds

You remember you are writing to the Queen

More equipped to handle the simpatico of worlds far between

And every time you shucked you

Every time you passed the buck

And so it is

The bringer of civilization is left amuck

Accounting too many strange fruits he can't unpluck

At once our forgiveness will call the cast

to mend evens and odds of jagged wrongs

Agree to live again

THE ABORTION

The full-blown massacre in me

That's what I feel

Scenes of prostitution

Lechery is what I invited to taste me

A feast within the jungle

Last night in a flash

I was there

The boar cornered me in that cave

Gouged my sides

Then from my navel

Licked me up

To whisper a care it could not find for me

The boar wanted to say

You side tracked me

Now the beast of it is what we have to heal

For the return,

We'll save our whole name.

PART TWO

BRING THY BREAD AND THY CUP

~

SPIRITUALS

D. F. Howard

CROSSING THE WATER

Defending my life, sustained over gravity
Obstinate wisdoms, implying my poverty

Play-picking me like I'm the sore
Hung-up in the boughs
Of New Age sedations that make haste
While placating my escape

Pleading for the words that I speak
Negating my containment
Inciting absences for the Cure
Grievous bylaws runnin' barefoot on the pavement
While layman cry relativity
So chaired to adversity
Yet, bound by the Married seat
Of Father, Son, and Spirit

Where being searched and being known
Can never distaste the quiet of being Owned

~

No, I have no respect for virtual reality
Aftertastes of Zen gardens and fallacies

Disheveled old men of the cloth
Shadowboxed by the lewdness that their heresy wrought

Proverbial botulism
Enmity eloped in prisons
Good Samaritans sitting down
As in the madness of gentle cows

When they throw hope down, obliterated

By wishing wells they have acquainted
They tune in to be slated
For this next aggression's bell
Now the topical living hell

Oh, but to tell

There's a Familiar Corps
Children that He foreswore
Conceptions that we implore
Free-ones of His demeanor
The gleaners
Waxing it out cleaner
Than the man in the arena[1]

In truth, yea, but in Spirit

For The Coming is supple
Earth, not granite
Nor fashions of stone

Don't just leave hope alone

Dispose of logic for
Nigh translated thought

Enoch being caught and taken up
By the Promise, for we've been sought
To transfigure naught into a sound
Of dear beloveds that have been found

A walk in the night

Betwixt the door
Of heaven's gate and earth's wide-open floor

---

[1] Thomsen, Brian M. *The Man in the Arena: Selected Writings of Theodore Roosevelt: A Reader*. By Theodore Roosevelt. New York: A Forge Book, 2003.

D. F. Howard

I found valiant men
Privileged-to-be-persecuted men
Patiently enduring kin
My own well-reputed friends

Basked in the bosom of Abraham's adore
Lovingly awaiting our eager rapport
For something that's more than just fated
Images of ourselves getting situated

Delivered from cursory accusations
Albeit, reprobate evaluations
Need I say, to compare ourselves to see
Who is it that'll be
The next angel of light that fell indeed

God did Nebuchadnezzar right
Bold in his displacement
The "Big Tree" Babylonite
Disowned to a beast
Cause self-praise was his feast
Masturbated beyond elated
Carrion turned to seed
For fowls who only eat
The exchange of His trust for greed

Whoa, it be a warrant to thieves

Still, cantors reverence man's bas-relief

Mocking the Sacred Injunction
For He gave us one function
To love Him, without interruption

Convey the Conversation

For Dominion is not a tower, it's in our hands
See, we were given the need for deep romance

It's time to be still
As a mild, gentle woman
Blushing, she gives her hand to her husband
Giving her response to what's in a man
Her simplicity un-wraps his loving command

The time to reveal
Without the need for remarks

Capsize, even, the dread of the dark

As I look to the breadth
Onward, and into the depths

The water implores my gait with its span
Rhapsody, alone awaits
I am

D. F. Howard

MAKING ME A WOMAN
(Ezekiel 19: for my beloved sisters)

The quilt given makes perfect sense to me now
Make me a woman

I can tell foolish pride what to do with destiny
It's not intricate that the key to my mystery is in Your mastery
My harbor has no room for chess players with jestful moves

Peeped in on them
Outside, making moves to sculpt me
Couldn't sleep in good flight
Hopped to and baked three cakes

Cried
Tickled pink
Cause I maintained my interpretation
Until they ate off only the icing

I am left
To concentrate
To think what to invent into next
Too soon to share the staircase to my righteous footing
Sometimes

My making veil is not just fine until all the colors convey my people's faculties

I'll eat that

For now my tiger cubs sleep under the will of my dear and latent warm

Making Me a Woman

Beulahland

<u>*The Diva*</u>
(Surrender)

i am here.

enhanced by this staff
myself

Austere
yet similar.

understand that He reaps for me

and just like that
my work is done.

NOT EVEN KNOWING IT

D. F. Howard

__HALLOWED WOMAN__

(Hallowed be her name)

A waif in time's thinned madness

She is not diminished

She is not without a finish

She is not without the need for a Holy joust

Although divested

Her heirloom

Divested

Throughout time's thinned madness

And the big bricks men have laid

She is dauntless

She is not phased

Regrouping within the Holy of Holies

She is His chambermaid

He has said

For naught of vanity

BE RICH

When you are finished, you will be pristine

A lion hunts a zebra in purity
As verity communes their flesh

The plainsman lived for this
Pursued the mighty buffalo for his morrow bliss
Reverencing
Even before the creature was slain
Beneath him
(Horizontal it seemed)

It was so that he would not just begin to feast
It was so that he would not eat in the least

Until his prayer ritual had enraptured the elevated mind of the beast
Not before would one morsel nor spite pass between
If the buffalo unto the Indian did not its spirit entreat

Oh, how we should adore
Instead of banning unseen Reality

Resign from this dry place
Bent on writing itself a plague

Today
Let's give ourselves to a more Excellent way

Be kind to Yourself
Do not say no
My Love

D. F. Howard

I'LL BEAR MY WINGS

In time
I wait
And bear my own

It humbles me
Inviting me Home

I nest
What stays with me is my soul's contest

My freedom is tuned to come
So nay
I say
My wait be undone

In time

I'll stake my claim
Until the battle in me is one and the same

No dis-ease
Negating me
Saying love and promise
Just in jest

In time
There will be no more suggestions
Persuading me
Crazing me
Evading me
Or calling me out my name

In time

I'll bring my Eventuality outside of me

In Spirit

I'll bear my wings

PART THREE

FINE TIME FOR THE ASKING

~

DAY TO DAY

D. F. Howard

<u>Rebellion</u>
(Man & Woman)

Living mostly outvoted
He often contrives by the will of his mind

Deafened, as heartless wisdom

With his mask affixed
His usual fears
Almost always
Steer him into more careers
Aloft from himself for years
While dreaming of fettered victims

      ~

Poetry is hers to ascertain

She lovingly removes any shackles that make them plain

Together they are well
Never beating an issue
Never going gray

They know better than to stray

Living the grace of conversation
Of whining they no longer have a need

No one is right or wrong

Dancing the dance of the Inevitable
They are strong

Their meaning being met

They do not regret

Heaven-made
Bedfellows
Partners
Engaged and working
In tune with the same rhythmic sunrise

In bloom and blooming

There's no telling what man and woman together can move

D. F. Howard

<u>Class Ring</u>
(in New Orleans)

remember ya girl

linzee

oh
nah that was a shame

yay huh

the one that gave it away to that stink boy

wutchamacallim
who mama had a lil money

yay yay
him

the one who couldn't even skate

him
yay
him

you rememba

anyway
po linzee

huh dingy self

must notuv even noticed the time that they started doing it

plus

she cuddah caughtem on wunnuhdim
good days

yay
cause you know
that boy's hygiene was on a strange rotation

yes indeed

look

an din

linzee's
cuzin
tole
me
that
the girl
thought he
lookdid cleen

well

we all tookum for cute on first sight too

look nah

linzee said
he was so well read

yeah right
you know as well as I do
that
that funkee lil ponk
knew what to say

plus

D. F. Howard

dat girl
wudunt
from
roun heah
no way

so
huh cuzin said
whin the girl
fownt out
that everybody nu

I mean
the peepul she nu

nu

the peepul she didn't know
nu

er body
nu

huh cuzin said

whin
linzee finelee lurnt it

the girl near bout went bline

(laughter)

damn
i feel like a krimnal
we krimnals
dat's just a damn krime
mhmm
po kummunakashun

puhsonofied

(breathless)

lissin nah

an
an
linzee
talking bout
she wondered why
he all but refused
tuh take off his shoes
aftuh
she hinted at it three different times

oh
ahn ahn

see
that
fonkee
lil boy
swoh he was wrong

nu
it was probably his only chance to get his swurv on

anyway aftuh it was wurl news

that po chile
jus
broke down

ran
jurned the convent

over on ponstince street

D. F. Howard

jus
finished school one day

whent an took
huh vowels

an frum that day on
she promised to give all her days to the holee sakruhment

I sweah
she right deh to this day

she evun cut off her own feet
so she could not run away

Quid Pro Quo

Smoker's
suffocating
integuments

Animals
assimilating
those who live to eat them

What do we believe in?

Cancer-bound
is the grievous man.

Hannibal

frequently

de-capped

the proposition

without using the words

What do we believe in?

Fractions

Slow

Down

Shelve your demands

Make the day fuller than the rants and the raves

The principal cause will always find you

Ticking you off

You will learn how to wait

<u>The Romantic</u>
(let it go)

how'd I come to be this place

peace never comes as I keep-sake

it's not like me to be this way

having doubts and feeling shame

but how to disown what I've maintained

D. F. Howard

Making Ends Meet

I
The synergist

I
Who makes futile
The synergism

I time the habitual synergy

In and about the mirage of voices
That skate and croon about

Always
The call that beckons me
Compels me to reach in and pull out my heartstrings

At arms length
At close range

All of it
Wants me to stop
And listen to what it needs
(They do not think it strange)

The only amino acid that is vital

Their eventuality on a high-pitched turn
There is no me

On
Under
The Syn

<u>*Flora Sounds Out Destination*</u>

i found

one black baby

and one flat shoe

I tripped

and landed this male placid dancer

who watched me

all through the night

and all through the day

standing closely behind me

constantly on the verge of all

his brand new truths

he has for me

D. F. Howard

Mono Gram

a sigh
long ago deserted

a weighed-down
tired listen

letting me know why you don't want to mix

relentlessly

devoted

is the winter

brought to me

by you

Enter: Secret

Her mystery is supported with the energy that only her whims can supply...Overtime she solicits grooms...many mates...programming songs, bongs, and many dedicated to what they knew as norm ...budding floral seeds whisper her work to diligent worker bees...their only mission is to admit her lure in life...their daily illustration...a perpetual eyes-glazed-over stick and buzz meditation...the neighborhood she keeps is scented by the trail of a special honey-sweet aptly placed between the shadows of homes...She vouches for anyone disowned, any pre-hassled judge and most ensuing grudges of the roundabout streets...Her inner circle has their work for the day...they make haste to circulate her taste 'less she escorts any man to their souls bound or faint...time and again she even uses her quiet image to seduce the verve of a butterfly's flutter and hop-in-gait...kissing with love and hate she is often dismayed...evermore encased by her wanton lusts for multiple things...she repeats her name...she longs to supply a relaxed state which the butterfly inadvertently claims...mounting the butterfly...now arrested with weight...they determine to lighten the load of another's day.

D. F. Howard

<u>Life</u>
(for June Babe)
I Peter 2:20

pain

soul-deepening

deliberate smiles

letting my mind recall

this happening

my father

had to tell me

his story

about

when he was a boy

and his pet pig he named Pete

about when

the time came for slaughter

he said

he could not let his friend

just go and become pig's feet

jelled up in any old jar

on some Mississippi juke joint bar

no

so he went right on over

and politely plucked his switch from the notorious apple tree

and so the lament

his father's standard thrashing

what's one more day

(big)

(fat)

(smile)

D. F. Howard

Spring's First Psalm

An Illumined place

An exquisite gleam delights my face

To you I will be shining

Inside the same Cardinal circle

We have been conveyed

My testimony to your endearments

To you I will be shining

Poetry Session

This is not me

Trying to catalog life or the credence of man

This is not me

Wanting to land you

I merely need to know

What being meek really means

D. F. Howard

<u>Wishful Thinking</u>

Often
Friends don't look like people who will try to take your choice from you
Inclined to feel this way
Icicles melt in the same way that people do
I often mean help
When I say
Really
I'm okay

Listening

Apart from the aloof dismissal masking my contrite
Your concern was committed to follow up my nonsense
Helping me to really make it alright

No sweat
I can stare straight into the noonday sun
For the longest time
Without batting an eye

The Victim Series

I can't lie anymore

'Less it's alright with you

It's stepping up to me

Give me a cause

Just one

To say it was heaven-sent

And I'll give this much to you

You can hear the frustration in my smile

But still

I love you

And that makes everything alright again

Doesn't it

Silly

D. F. Howard

<u>*Laughing*</u>

The time I got there late

The time that could not wait

While choking on hate

I saw myself lapsing

One five-pointed mound

Recapping

The places

I sat seething in my multiple self-lashings

Now, this time

With unforeseen agility

I brought it back

Laughing

You'll Ascend

You see

You have no rhyme

In making it happen

You're not breathing in aware

The music I'm sending has both meter and time

Shame or Pride

Cannot save the day

Face it and then you'll shine

Hit-home emotions have eternity's gain in mind

And what an ascent

To live inside The Flame

I am not just some piper

Hot to blow your horn

In search of my fame

You are the image of my face

And I'll never forget you

So, be not blind to your own deceit

D. F. Howard

Armed with desperate tragedy to complete

Get out of your own way

And let yourselves see

The distinct Harmony laid at your feet

And what an ascent

The therapy your banished side could never contain

You were never some musical storm

Your play palace

Your fortress

Will never be the base

As you insist upon defending your case

Meanwhile

The Wait

And what is to come

Be it not the same boring song

Ascend with Me

I am your ground

Settled within

Fruitful trees

There is much to see

Every artist has come to Me for a movie

Ascend

Worship in Truth

So your mountain to climb

Will continue the dawn at root

For that which is Everlasting in you

Brethren, live this majesty

Be not bound by Herod's feet

PART FOUR

AUTUMNS CONVERSATION WITH BLISS

~

REVELATIONS

D. F. Howard

Love and Numbers

Totals of you

I was promised to complete

So I longed 'til you rode your wave

Chief commander of matrimony

On this priestly ship

We sail

Cardinal air follows our indigo

In bliss

Every whole of you is me

Bandits of kind butter

Timeless

<u>Behold</u>
(the inner life of a child)

Behold

She turns to me
A creature well-fashioned
Sneaking in all her little peeks
As she's lulled to sleep

This baby I see
Features me
And my eyes
And my Home
Viewing me

Unresolved
She dreams
Laughin'
Kinda' half-grinnin'

She is akin me
She blends me

Nestled within the mild rocking of my inseams
To and fro
She moves closer within
Enveloped by the deepest R.E.M.
She surpasses time and space
As I look on with patient grace

So endearing
She suckles

Curdlin' Mammae
Curdlin' the milk that is her mold

D. F. Howard

My child is now restin' in between what is seen
Where she often bends and leans

She is adrift
And begins to transmit her innate Ujai breath

So intent

Showing us how to circumvent the spiraling unseen
Of too many dimensions unredeemed

She swims with ease
Through the ancient-most seas
And their red-orange dips
Contemplating trips around olden drums afire

Her amber-hot looms
Her two irises ogle
Allied
She is Granmama-Astro-Ole'
And so often finds a retreat
For those who can't take the heat

Her burlap garments and shackles are shed
Uncloaked
She fancies herself
Not led by foreign names
Bought to brand her
For toil in cotton to cane

She is here
Olden still
In between divisions
Of prominent boats and bodies set to motion
Through waters of travailed emotion

Exposed tribes and their visions
Left to a griot's timeless precision

She is so cool
Already, she has learned to master this cruise
Right past nostalgia's crave
Right past confusion's plague

She's alive
Her spirit zests
Packed with live enzymes
That tend to test
And tap dance non-recluse

Deliberately she reviews the songs of our soul

With healthy intentions towards her mission
Now made true in foretold depictions

My Spirited child
Candid and cute
Has the ability
The eye for humanity
The infrared eye that sees
The seer kind
That suspends disbelief
For the Father's heart she aims to keep
And means she will entreat the semblance of one's own Identity

She was born
To align the plot
Inviting all those to meat
To sup with the Enlightened Lot
The washing of hands and then of feet
Divinely, tying the knot of man and Peace

From bygone to bygones
Through eons on end
Chirin'-Cosmo-Scientifica heals
And is healed

D. F. Howard

They all make amends

Continually
My daughter strokes through the whey
Invoking her mother

She is hope, His glory
Evermore
Everyday

Of yore
It is her visage
Gleaming

Coaxing hymns and victory songs

Tot-Impressionistica

Running-Naked is sound
For He is with us now

It is truth to be seen
She is the only reason He gave breast to me

We are gathered unto Him of Benevolent things

Yoghurt clapped in no sound

T'aint a fuss in us

She sleepin'

Overlapped

<u>Scribes Spoke Sage</u>
(a legacy)

Burn this page
And the blood runs free
In pools

Flash your pass
If you are suited for this writ unclaimed

It is dominion
Solace and fortitude
The knowing
The prize
In between winning a dime
Where and all the twains do meet

The action is one of alchemy
Converting the old
The accustomed to things
Whereby you find the means
To hone all those unrequited extremes

Since ancient times
Betrothed variations that can't be quelled
The prosperity of a people is what's compelled

Therein
Your word
Your bond

Let's you in
Amidst the quiet of a perfect page

Seeking the cost of possibility
Ever-finding is the servant

D. F. Howard

The scribe
Diligently preparing the access of true tidings
Emitting many truths never spoken
Looking into the indiscriminate eye which transcends laziness
And those that wallow in their comfort confines

Transcending oxygen is the sage

Passing through this intermediate wilderness
Where one laps while sitting in wanderlust
It is the scribe that writes us through the ruff

Inviting us beyond our linear selves
So oft we've been crowned, then abased

Yet, His spirit quickens us to preserve The Race

Awakened, He transfuses our vitality with His grace

The scribe inhales this oxygen
And replenishes what patiently awaits
For the moment perpetually on the move
Is the wisdom to want the truth
And the chase which never degrades
Papers Available Inside Your Store

<u>*Washed Ashore*</u>

(blessings in disguise)

Making a vow

To see Him above me

Coming down to don me

Preparing me for purity

My honest ascension

From time and place

To a Surety never-ending

Adoring is my gratitude

There's something to be said of The Shore

D. F. Howard

Portrait of Toms

(too many uncles)

The Great Willow sheds her skin for the umpteenth time

She had seen malignancy in your eyes

Leaving you to deny
Leaving you to break off The Rib
Just above the importance of your right thigh

Feeling some sentence was passed (on her)
You'd often sigh

Between all of your fleeting spits of bile
You were left in obvious denial

Never demising
Your reserved inanity

And with it
You forged right ahead
Naming her the inferior calamity

Regardless
She could still find her smile
Throughout all your infamous witch trials

And it comes to this
You scheme to court her

Ultimately
To make her the blame

The blame
For being the embodiment of what was taken from you

The blame

Because everyday
In every way
She single-handedly exhibits you to yourself

(As if she doesn't Belong)

It was small
But I can recall
There was a Muslim/ woman/ mother/ wife
Who made the news the other day

A woman
Who on a normal day
And in a normal way
Walked along in the usual marketplace

And with a woman's innate grace
While attempting to smell a piece of fruit, she lifts her veil

When she does this
Just one smidgen above her chin
She reveals a secret, little bit of skin

Well the vendor/ storekeeper saw her
And to her husband
He told of her
Of how she lifted her veil
Going against the consistency of their rigid laws

Enforcing it
The storekeeper insisted that she was a whore to be sent to hell

Simply because she lifted her veil
Simply because she wanted to smell

D. F. Howard

To smell
Something so innate of a woman's grace
At least when dealing with food everyday, anyway

So her husband
Having gotten this big wiff
Of the same inane scent that got the vendor all taut and out-of-shape and bent

The very same scent got the husband's mouth ready and set to taste her being the blame
For his nightly and daily urges to rediscover himself within the female mystery

The very act alone reveals his lust
And the accountability of his lowest degree,
Vexing them to flee the garden they could no longer see

When she reacted in haste and prompted The Fall
He felt he was her subordinate, her employee and all

Branded, a vagrant to all theosophy

Juxtaposed was her as the entity
The evidence of his integrity left naked to the thief

Beautiful work and worship cheapened by the fraud
Who extracted them from Eden and God

Repackaged in shame and blinded now
With no convictions his lurking desire found no restrictions
In having the need
To be driven up
Back into the womb
To be attached to the Rib
That once for him said Home

Finally, devising the morbid wile of his driving tool
He knows not to panic
Knows not to let the cat out of the bag
Knows not to let her know

The nostalgic and respective service of her inside room
And those flowering roots that know just how to soothe

Roots with no like kinds
Each vintage having its own personality
Each woman's crop growing its own finality

Knowing this, he worries
That eventually she'll come to realize
And relive the doom every time they fantasize

So he's born
Trained to distract her mind from discovery
Keeping her from information
And the truth between their lives
Not responding to her as tender and kind

Instead man faces the origin of black
Inherited by death, he's filled with lack

Esteeming threats under his seat to bring demise
Not her, not anyone will soften his guise
No room is given for other plans to be devised
No one will tear the roof off his enterprise

The Capital of Masochism has been contrived
It has declared its position as righteous
In it the men have presented themselves as Titans
Defending their definitive weak reply
Leading all of humanity into despair without questioning why

The men are drench with what their grieving
Insecurity festered from "the author of lies"
Men are seething, because they accepted sin while sleeping

Hurt that's paranoid, he disguises with bile
Displaying power, to sow all his wiles
So, he combs every chance to chastise her smile

D. F. Howard

Tripping over himself, he becomes the drone
Of doctrines dealing in the demonstration of his feelings

More than ever, he's being honed to repress her inception of God alone

Because she was blessed with the power to love, to change, and to Spiritually exchange

And that she is a master in her own rite
Born to complement, and give birth to his life

To touch the inside of him
She wants to nurture his Inner Life

Giving him favor with man and God
She lives to remove feelings of abandonment and strife
Fulfilling prophecy, a wife

She is one to commend

Instead, she is defaced with suggestions that veils recommend
Disguising her as a seemingly chaste one
As one betoken

She is a master
Standing alone, and laying down
Her body is the land of the King's Own Crown
Adorned for appreciation, not to be conquered by an ox

Her name is Beautiful,
Supreme Submission
Multiplying dreams and hope and Vision

She is a Helpmeet
Without the intentions of his too many elders
Calling themselves moral leaders
Who crave so badly to purify and keep her

As it is now
It was then

For example,
The Salem witchtrialers

Witchtrialers
Disguising themselves as damn fruit vendors
Storekeepers
Watchers
Watching her
Watch her husband
Watching the hottest fire

As it consumes her

He thinks he means to purge her
Simply because she lifted her veil

When it was just a piece of fruit she aimed to smell

To smell
A respectful, natural gesture for a woman
In her state of grace

At least when dealing with food everyday, anyway

Now in the name of his god
He intends to send her flesh and soul to hell

Did a trial ensue
Was he acquitted
Having been found "falsely accused"

It
Not being murder
But it being justice

D. F. Howard

After all, a major rule had been broken

There was no discourse; she was to be a token

So, the one misused
The one made to be a muse in talking about this dynamic blame
Now centrifuged

Her name still goes unspoken

~~~

As usual the Great Willow looks on at man in humanity
Man who is hell-bent to disdain his Vitality

She looks on as man adopts his belief systems adamantly

And so it is

The Willing Willow finds her state of grace
In her ability to exfoliate

Sloughing off his frank denials
Sloughing off his spits of bile
Sloughing off his belief systems for hire

She still stands
She humbly accepts His power
She is lithesome
Much strength she has acquired

Hers to possess
Hers to exceed unrest

She is admired

She is never too tired
To help or to inspire

Those many Toms
(her too many uncles)

All of them who spit and drink in the mire

No, she never tires of watching them

Seemingly of their free will
Seemingly to help balance the bill
Seemingly to help the Great Willow scratch her back

So, in turn, she'll be moved to scratch his

Her too-many-uncles go through the motions

He gestures to comfort her
As she sheds her skin

Just in time for her to grimace
Then looking away from him
She responds to the itchiest itch

Just long enough for him to slip in

In sufficient time for him to Revisit the exact Rib
That was taken out of him way back when

By hook or by crook,
He goes through all of that just to get back in

D. F. Howard

<u>*The Birds and the Bees*</u>

Two blocks of wood

One misshapen dagger

Tanned cowhide canvassing my shoes

Shoes equipped for anything

That could be qualified as a natural disaster

Or all-in-a-day-type situations

Come to find me

Reasoning with this reality

Based on capturing

Displaced

<u>*Triple Blue*</u>

(…and His voice as the sound of many waters… Rev 1:15)

It is pleasant
It's bliss kissing fellow man

Wanting to know
It longs to see us along the sands

The Big Blue
A devoted fan
Waves with its consistent hand to gather the conclusion unknown by man

With boldness it spoke
To reveal the many veils we've cloaked
As it maintains the timeless refrain

If you could, would you keep this for tomorrow's moon

With this at hand
How to say
How to display
This to all of man
Having coined it a wicked, well-stormed plan

What is more, too many ills were oft ashore
Whence last the Great Reef was tore

The Late Great Tore
Readjusting our core
Shifting to situate the new continent floors

And since then, it stands
We are not convinced to intercede dry lands

Now with this understanding

D. F. Howard

And thinking to know this truth

He's blessed the day that we swoon

If you could, would you keep this for tomorrow's moon

Don't be appeased by me
This is the path to our victory

If you depend on your humanity as your only strategy
Then the duel and you go hand in hand
Leaving on hold this life manifold

Triple threats
Full-blown
Endlessly will be sown
By you
Ensued and encased by your own rage

He says: If you would only give it to Me

On one hand, that same rage can extol The Deliverer
By divulging all misleading fantasies
That beckons every thief to a look-see
On the same hand, you can slay the iniquity of your cold theories with irrational faith

Rage, feeling it's being beseeched knows to alert you, its owner
And awaken you, its master
So, you can go and tell the land-ones, the unconvinced-ones
The can't—stand-too-close-to—the-shore-ones

Rage will show up to tell you, its governor, to realize its proper use

Then, you'll convey this to those that don't believe
Helping them to know how and why the Ocean soothes

Eventually, you'll be reproved
Moving from desolate lands onto Bridled shores

Standing in the Quiet of the Blue Unmoved

You'll begin to accept
You'll begin to adore

The next, pleasant visit
Of the Late Great Tore
Kept just in time for the Appointed moon

Lovingly attuned and confessing, you'll swoon
Romanced by the kiss of the Comforter's bliss

Repletion is the Lord's rapport
Drawing many to wade along the shore
In His Rest, you'll believe with outstretched hands
Satiated, you'll love His Unconditional Command

Appreciating

Triple Blue

PART FIVE

EVEN TUNDRAS CAN CIRCULATE HEAT

~

EXPANSION: SUPERNATURAL

D. F. Howard

Mothering: Seeds of Three Through Ether

I received three blindfolds in the mail yesterday
Two fit, but the other I nearly threw away
Within moments there was a tap on my sun-roof window pane
I gently opened it to challenge my nerve
Then a bird gave forth information of Teresa's mother passing away

Within those seven seconds, I paused to reminisce about the sweet-marrow Mrs.
Who witnessed my growth, and watched me style my youthful glow
Accompanied by my usual seas of anguish

She comforted me, just with her listening
Then, she'd give me anecdotes that have steadied the person that I am today

I supplied at her counter oftentimes
She would bake anything for me: cakes, cobblers, pies

She'd have on-hand sour or crumbly treats I'd crave

Making, being- alive on Saturday to Sunday evenings a quaint, protected holiday

Now I am here to give a graceful farewell to Mrs. Esther
The mother who could communicate her light as she saw into my life

We will talk more
She would humbly offer me
Whenever my burden to pray led me to question if I really wanted to walk in the new-
found responsibility

As you minister
It discloses the unseen
Then the light from this gives strength
And conveys a new song to everything

I am a child of this

There, the Holy Spirit labors with me

Your gift will always tie in dimensions
As you agree, it will sustain, for you are one and the same

You know the place I'm speaking of
When you witnessed them
With majesty they called His name

Now, you'll visit this place again

From now on, when you see the structure of Ethos, just begin to pray

As you continue to exclaim
A glimpse of your Dominion will be proclaimed

Sleep there
Eat there

This nourishment will warm your womb for intentions you'll bear again

As you comply with the unfolding message

It will enliven your home

Remember, He will guide you with His eye, not deny you

Then, you shall find the Truest Love

Undefiled

That you could never retain

D. F. Howard

N.O.L.A.: L'eau Reflexology

(monologue of home)

Prefixes
On all my babies

On 'em
For 'em

I watch from inside
I see them foil
Though I never tremble

My lil' shorties
Are sensing to play more tricks
To get themselves away
From the shotgun homes
That keeps them smirking in between their pouts

Always runnin' hard, like lil' storms
Huffin' and puffin'
Breathing hard-kept hurt

In storms they take over the house
Smellin' like sweaty little puppies

But they are still my papoose manaetas

That's just my pet name for these children who are my everything

Anyway
Today's the day
That they catch wind of all their lil' faullies an' 'nem
Boutah' go see The 'Gras Indians

Yeah

They gon' buck jump
An' strut `a la Treme

Gon' did it
Done did it

An' they call theyself gettin' over on me

An' all that energy
Where they gets it
'Specially my third and my ninth one

Them chirin' is my spitten' image
It's scary

I remember mama use to say

Queen, girl you know you spat them chirins' out
Couldn't deny 'em if you wanted to

Nah, you boutah' see what you put me thu'

Ah hee hee hee

Tole' ya' I was gon' get ma' nuff

Nah, here they come
Scufflin' on my poach'
Playing them checkers
And jumpin' double-dutch for days

But I make 'em go 'cause they don't want to do nothing else
Carryin' on like they bewitched
And trying to charm me out of everything

They say
I thought this was owwa' day

D. F. Howard

I say
I ain't gon' let cha'll out- talk me

See, ya'll think just cuz' ya' Nanneh and Pareinh over here
Then ya'll gon' have your way

They become still when I say this
They wait
Bearing the sound of me talkin'
Waiting for my mind to change

Then, they stage another performance to say what they want to say

I say
Jus' go on head Nanneh
'Cause, see
Ya'll done spoiltem' rotten
An' I gotstah' stay

They keep on cuttin' up
Performin' 'til they gets their way
Throwing all kinds of fits
Passionately convincing me to play

My babies
Look at 'em

Mother wit, is what they call it
Keeping me steady all these days

It's too soon ta' really say about 'em
These chirin' are too wild for nature

Still
They're just models in this plague

~~~~~~~~~~~~~~~~

Once, my father blest this city

On account of its seafood burls
Cookouts
Shouts

After-school children eatin' pig lips with potato chips
Supplementin' them early on

Loud and common, lady-sassies
Hollerin' at those sometimey' daddies with sock-it-to-me spice

Everybody's voice ringin' throughout these narrow streets
with that Nawlins twang

Now, this one an' that one wannabe kintuh' the friend
they just met on Fat Tuesday
To pass over what they already got

Cause sometimes ya' too "black" or too "bright" in ya' skin to be in their spot

But still, it's this confused lil' town

Now
Lookin' around
It's obvious ta' me

I see The Waits inside all us babies
An' 'nat's alright
'Cause He's sergin' up through the roots
All
Up
In
Our searchin'

I see 'em
They stay out for long spells
Tappin' their shoes on liquor street

D. F. Howard

But the Bourbon can't refill what their missin'

And it's not under the water
We don't need the Scorpion fleet
No revisitin' Atlantis
Ya' heard meh'

Them type of waves can't heal my babies
Or refurbish their pangs

An' 'nat's why New 'Erlins sangs
An' marches
Its' tribes and churches
An' lives- to- eat
To meet and feed
Any and all people transplanted here

The ones that come here to dwell
Wide-eyed and open

They come to re-supply
Where they feel they lost something
An' think it's here

An' they swear she's alive
An' lurkin'
Then, they make-believe
They run to a dead woman: making wishes and XXX up her grave

They just want what they want
Live or Die

Even if she's a lie

'Cause Sambo, Sambo was the word

But, this Crescent City is waiting for the "Risin' Sun"
To bring the peace we can't find from no big, white bird

Alright

An' nat's why I don't mind too much when my chirin' try gettin' over on me
Alright

Them ma' papoose manaetas
Alright

And they gon' be fine

So, Nannenh an' Pareinh

Go right on 'head

I see how ya'll help my babies to savor life
Like they suckin' all the taste outtuh' creamy prailine

They deserve the right to be as sweet and meek and nutty as they wannabe

I pays attention to them: Grinnin' they teeth is all of them onlookers
Passing by the crowded spots

They throw down monies to glimpse a taste of our rare-a-sweet goodies
Watching our chirin' dance their dance
Them tourists couldn't, even, begin to understand
'Cause it cost them chirin' something to dance like that

And they didn't buy it from no man

So, go on 'head Nannenh
Ya'll spurl 'em
I don't mind

'Cause ya'll say godmother and godfather outtuh' sugar-love
An' that's all mine

So, yeah, we pressing through

D. F. Howard

Ma' papoose manaetas
Me
Lagniappe
Plus roots

Reapin' on, even aftuh' Easter
An' church bells
An' tourist spells

All us
We are the natives, waiting for what He said

Oh, yeah
It's soon ta' be
Oh, it's comin' to a head

Nah', be a witness

His Beautiful Name gon' be said
Sung
'Birfed
Rebrassed and fonked
Throughout the Quarter
From up-above the Dome
Even through the slap an' catch-back-hooks
Of them gator claws

Oh yeah, He gon' come

Down in New 'Erlins
Nuttin' but smellin' salts
Grounding feets
Stompin' through
Fencin' ta' move all us babies in just awhile

Then we gon' pronounce: Love has come from Thee

The Sanctuary

The night-sending moon
Illuminated
Barebacked
We pray

Reverent

We stay

Life mid-symphony

We pray

Souls on the limb

Initiate oneness

Again
Begin

D. F. Howard

The Rebirth of Cool

(In response to Poe and the land of Oz)

Twilight kindred to a poet black

Epitaphs entomb our bended backs

By which our motives stand

Beguiled by the words of everyman

Seeking solace in our image

Then, our fame becomes undone

Peradventure

By reason of The One

Whose motions lend His motions style

The One Who bestows us the Color

Conveys us the Noun

Lamenting

The Votive we've brandished and bound

So that, our bold, barren houses soften to bow

Since the "Quoth of Nevermore"
From the ravens…and the sadness
And "there's no place like Home."

After Word

This parable came to me seven years ago. Until the completion of this book, the interpretation had not been revealed:

A teenage girl in an African village becomes deathly ill. She has a very high fever that will not break and continues to sweat profusely, despite any traditional treatments offered by her mother. The girl trembles involuntarily, and becomes despondent although she exhibits normal functions such as walking. She will die in a matter of days, unless a remedy is administered to her.

Feeling helpless, her parents accompany her to town in hopes of some intervention. As they approach the village square, they encounter a scaffold that has been erected amidst many curious onlookers. At that moment the griot made an announcement, drawing a handful of the people closer to the scene, but most of them shrink back to watch from afar. The girl's father approaches the man and speaks with him for a time- an agreement is obviously made. He returns to the girl and her mother. As the father comforts his daughter, he engages her with firm words of counsel, causing her to weep.

Two men enter along side a lion that is not leashed or controlled in any way. As it waits behind the platform, the girl grievingly approaches the structure and climbs the steps. The two men help her onto a center block and proceed to make the necessary adjustments in positioning her. Her mother and father look on in despair to that which must be unseemly. After the coital transmission the child's symptoms did subside and a resolute calm remained with her…as the lion passed away, she held his mane and spoke with him.

www.ingramcontent.com/pod-product-compliance
Lightning Source LLC
Chambersburg PA
CBHW030354290526
45785CB00004B/1750